ZOLA LEVITT PRESS

Whose Land Is It?

Study Booklet & Transcripts

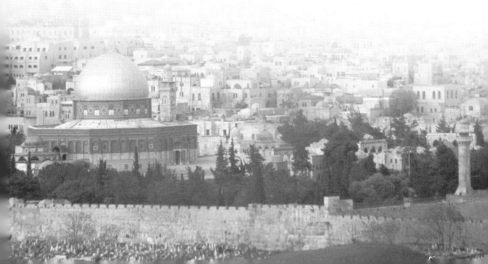

© 2003 by
Zola Levitt Ministries, Inc.

All rights reserved. No part of this transcript may be reproduced in any form without permission from the publisher, except in the case of brief quotations embodied in critical articles or reviews.

ISBN: 1-930749-42-2

Printed in the United States of America

Contents

Whose Land Is It? 5

The View from Palestine 23

Whose Land Is It?

Transcript from the Original
Zola Levitt Presents Program

Zola Levitt

Whose Land Is It?

> This is a transcript of a spoken lesson, and we wanted to remain faithful to the verbal text. Slight editings for clarity have been made. Allowances should be made for the fact that spoken language reads differently than literary text.

Whose Land Is It?

I am going to discuss a subject that I think needs discussing. On college campuses today, universities, and every place, there is a kind of an anti-Israel divestiture movement, anti-Jewish movement, anti-Semitism, and so forth, all based on the idea that somehow the Jews are occupying the country of Israel, and it's really Arab land and belongs to Palestinian people. It's because the thing just isn't true – what's being published in the media, what's being said on campus often is simply not the truth – that this discussion is necessary.

Now, there are four points to Jewish ownership of Israel, and the whole question of the Jewish ownership of Israel.

First of all, they are the only people in the world with a land grant to the Land of Israel. Of course the land grant is in the Bible, and many people don't appreciate the Bible. But let me point out that the book of Genesis, in which the land was given to the Jews, is repeated in the Dead Sea Scrolls that were

Whose Land Is It?

found in caves in Israel and carbon dated at 200 BC. And they repeat the land grant. In other words, one doesn't have to believe the Bible. This is an ancient find. This is archaeology. And there in plain writing is the idea that the Jewish people get the land of Israel.

You don't, again, have to even believe that it's true. You only have to believe there were Jewish people, there was a Land of Israel, and it was given to them. That is, even if it was fiction, someone wrote it down and gave a title to some people called Jews of the country of Israel. And the whole world recognizes this conception of prior title. That is, the Dead Sea Scrolls were written, as I say, in 200 BC. Mohammed was not to be born until about 600 AD. That's 800 years later. There's no question of what title is prior. The Jewish title is prior. The idea that native people are in a land immediately implies prior title. In the United States in our history, we have native people here. We call them Indians and so forth. But their real name, and we call it that today, is Native Americans, because we all admit they were here first. They have real title to this land, even though it was taken from them and we occupied it. They were the original. The Indians were never called occupiers. When our pioneers went out west, most certainly they didn't write to Washington and say, "We're having problems out here. The Indians are trying to occupy this land." The Indians came with the land. They also did not report that the Indians were set-

Whose Land Is It?

tlers. That doesn't make any sense.

Now, likewise in Israel, the Israelis are the Indians, so to speak. They are the native people, the oldest people by far. If the Bible is to be believed at all, then they were there for thousands of years. But we don't have to rely on the Bible. I'm going to presently discuss the history of the place, the archaeology that has been found, and so forth.

But if one doesn't hold to the Scriptures, one would go then to secular history and would find the same thing – that the Jews are native to the land. When I say native, that is they are the first people building structures, settling the place after nomads, after Canaanites, Jebusites, people of that sort. They were there essentially first. But they were not Arabs at all. There were no Arabs in the land for centuries later. So the Jewish people are actually the originals, and they have the grant to the land. I want to point out that in this entire world of more than 200 nations, no other people has any kind of a grant to their land. Not a religious grant, or even a fictional grant, or a fable grant. No kind. The Jewish people are the only one with a grant to the land, and that grant is to the Land of Israel. It's clear.

Now when it was given, at least scripturally, it was given far more land than the Jews hold today; not just simply the West Bank, Gaza, the Golan Heights. The grant, if the Scripture is to believed, reaches

Whose Land Is It?

from the Wadi El Arish in the Sinai desert completely over to the Euphrates River on the northeastern side of Israel, taking in even the city of Damascus, most of Jordan, the southern areas of deserts, and so on. It's much larger as given to the Jewish people than they have today. It's a significant point, when you think of it, that they are settling for far less than they were given, and even this is attempted to be denied them.

Now, to the history. Let's suppose someone said, "OK. Scripture is simply Jewish writing, and of course it's partisan to them. They probably have edited it a hundred times, changed things around," if you like. Although you can't say that from the time of the Dead Sea Scrolls on, where there's a complete copy of Scripture, except for the book of Esther, the entire history books of Genesis, land grant, and all of it is in the Dead Sea Scrolls. Those are written materials. They cannot have been faked. They've been carbon dated. So, you have to settle that in 200 BC they did have a grant. But even before that, Greek historians, Roman historians observed that the Jews occupied the Land of Israel. It was Jewish land. There's no question of it. I have here a copy of a Roman history book, *Josephus, The Essential Writings*. It says on the cover, "An Illustrated Edition of Jewish Antiquities and the Jewish War." It doesn't say anything about Arab antiquities or Arab wars because they were not yet [there] at the time of Josephus, who was a Romanized his-

Whose Land Is It?

torian of the first century. There were no Palestinians to speak of. There simply were no Palestinians in this world. The country was named Palestine by the Emperor Hadrian in 135 AD, later than Josephus. But again, there were no Arabs involved. The Romans picked the name because it related to the ancient Philistines, enemies perennially of Jewish people. And it was another one of those final solutions to the Jewish problem. The fact is the Palestinians had nothing to do with the Arabs. They were Greeks. They came from the Adriatic areas and from Cypress. They pursued marine ventures along the coastlands of the east, everywhere in the Middle East. They were in Tyre, Sidon, down through Gaza, and so forth. And they oftentimes fought with the people inland to protect their investments, and so on. But there were no Arabs involved in this. Not until the birth of Mohammed did the Arabs begin to take an interest in the countries around them. And, of course, Israel was one of those. But they did not, of course, call themselves Palestinians then. The fact is the Arabs did not call themselves Palestinians until 1964 AD. In 1948, for example, the Jewish people were known as Palestinians and the Arabs rejected the name. They did not want to be called Palestinians. That was a Jewish terminology.

The story is told that Palestinian farmers went to California in the 19th century to show farmers in California how to plant vineyards, and to cultivate a land that is very much like Israeli land, a land of

Whose Land Is It?

mountains, deserts, various climates, almost semi-tropical, arid in some places. And they showed them how to plant the vineyards and so on, and the story is true. But all of those Palestinian farmers were Jewish. There was no indigenous Palestinian culture, no government, no country. A legitimate government leaves things behind. There are no documents, no currency, no legal forms, no stationery, if you will. No nothing. This is completely a modern people, if it's a people at all. In reality, the Palestinians are made up of Arabs who came across the borders principally since 1948, when the Jews started to build a modern nation. It happens in many places in the world. It happened here in Texas, and in California, where Mexicans came to take jobs and Central Americans, and so on; in Florida, where Cubans came. And the workers are welcome. They're paid a day's wage for a day's work. Their work is needed. They are usually skillful and cooperative, and so they were here in America.

As the Arabs came into Israel, they at first were skillful and cooperative, and then began to chafe under what they call an occupation. Of course, it was not an occupation. The Jews had simply returned to their native land.

Well, I'm going to come back after this with some talk about the archaeology that determines ownership of land. And also the principle by which we American immigrants, we white, black and yellow

Whose Land Is It?

people, occupy this continent – military conquest. I'll be back.

– – – –

Our tours of Israel have continued for thirty years. I took the first one in 1973, and frankly this is where I picked up the knowledge of the place, I suppose. I've always been a student of the Bible. In all that travel in Israel, talking to people on all sides of this question, by the way, including Palestinian Authorities like Faisal Husseini, Hanan Ashrawi, journalists and so on, people on the street, merchants, and, of course, the Israeli people, I guess I've learned a lot, and I'm absolutely shocked by what's going on on our campuses and in our newspapers. There seems to be almost no attempt to give a truthful estimation of what's going on over there.

I said I'd discuss the archaeology, and so on. That's a fascinating part of Israel. This is something Americans simply don't have, which is thousands of years of history in the ground. We have it in terms of finding an Indian buried 10,000 years ago, as it was said, or a burial ground usually more recent, arrowheads, tomahawks, etc. That's about the history that we can find here.

But in Israel we find history of ancient civilizations even predating King Solomon, King David, and so on. Recently an archaeologist on our program, Ian Stern, told me that they have found in the City of

Whose Land Is It?

David, which is a hillside beneath the southern wall of the temple platform, large pillars, big massive pillars from the time of Abraham, 10 or 15 feet high. This is some building for a few thousand BC! Four thousand years ago a lot of the world was still living in the forests. In Israel, people were building structures.

And Abraham apparently saw these pillars. And it clears up something of a mystery. The Bible story is that Abraham was to take Isaac to Mount Moriah and offer him in sacrifice. I think everybody in the world must know this story. But how did he find this particular mountain? Well, they came from Beersheba, from the southern side of Jerusalem, and must have entered the city over a hill that is now called the Promenade, from where you can view the city of Jerusalem. Walking straight toward what is now the Temple Mount, they would have come in to the bottom of what, a thousand years after Abraham, became the City of David. And right there the pillars stood, apparently, because they have fallen where they stood. And so they've been identified as belonging to the time. Now when Abraham saw those, he must have headed straight there. And from there on up the hill is the temple platform, and undoubtedly he would have walked up that hill to offer his son in sacrifice, because in those days the worship place was called a high place, and it was always the hill above the city and looked down on all the people. Whatever house of worship there

Whose Land Is It?

was, a grove or altar was put up on this high hill above the city. And from the City of David, that is the hill one sees – Mount Moriah. The Mount of Olives is on one side, it's higher. Mount Zion is on this side. But from the City of David, straight up the hill is the high place evidently for that civilization. And Abraham found it, and Scripture indicates the priest Melchizedek and personalities like him. But that's Scripture.

OK. What was found in the ground (that's certain archaeology, whether you believe scripture or not) are altars from Joshua's time with ancient Hebrew writing, and a stone proving the House of David. It says in plain Aramaic, and I can even read it. It's very clear, "the House of David." Scholars have for centuries said that David is a mythical figure, sort of like Homer or Ulysses, heroes in mythology, whatever, and didn't really live. He was about that same time.

I remember when I went to college. I went to Indiana University and I was studying for a doctorate there. I learned that King David was at the same time as the Greek mythology, and he was probably a mythological character. Well, that's not true. A stone with "the House of David" written on it, just as the Bible specifies, is extant from about 800 BC. David must have lived 150 years or so before that. This stone was carved by an enemy of Israel, the country to the north with whom they were at war;

Whose Land Is It?

but carved in the Aramaic language so that it's clear to read. So that is evidence that David existed. Easily you see these two pieces of archaeology: an altar from Joshua's time in Hebrew writing, and a stone from David's time with "House of David" written in Aramaic, which the Jews also used, are foolproof [testimony] of Jewish primacy in the land as of 3,500 years ago and 3,000 years ago.

Now, the Dead Sea Scrolls, they are one of the archaeological finds of all time. That is, one wants to find writing in the ground. That's wonderful.

When we found the Rosetta stone in Egypt, we broke the code and were able to read hieroglyphics in other languages readily. And I examined the Rosetta stone. It's in the British Museum. It's a large piece of stone with clear writing on it. It's only one stone with about four paragraphs of writing. The Dead Sea Scrolls are voluminous. Scroll after scroll after scroll, the entire Bible, other novels, an allegory of the battle of the sons of light and the sons of darkness. All these things from before the first century and for 50 years afterwards are written down in Hebrew. And this again proves the primacy of the Jewish people in the land. Then the cities that were built... my goodness, they have Biblical names. Nazareth, Bethlehem, Jerusalem obviously are Jewish cities. Arabs live in all three and are welcome, more or less, because of the times.

Whose Land Is It?

But look, those are Jewish cities that have Bible names. That's all there is to that. The Arabs did not build those cities, or most any city in Israel. Jerusalem is of particular controversy because the Jews claim it, of course, is their capital, and it always was. But Muslims claim it, too. But Jerusalem is not given in the Koran. It's not mentioned even once. It's mentioned more than 700 times in the Bible. The [claimed] reference to Jerusalem [in the Koran] is a reference to Al-Quds, the farthest mosque, a place distant from Mecca, is all we can ascertain. You could have picked almost any city. And I have a feeling Jerusalem was chosen by interpreters simply because Israel has been the hard nut to crack in the Middle East. The Arabs have come out of Saudi Arabia, conquered twenty-two Middle Eastern nations. But they never really have been able to put the Jews out of Israel. When the Jews were away in dispersion, people could come and occupy, and sundry people did from every place, from all countries around the Middle East.

But when the Jews returned in 1948 – by the way singing the same songs and praying the same prayers as they did when they were there 3,000 years ago – then Jerusalem was Jewish again, and they have persisted there. If the Bible had only one prophecy, that the Jews would be dispersed and nearly 2,000 years later return to their land, it would be a valuable book of prophecy. It would be something to reckon with.

Whose Land Is It?

Now archaeology is foolproof. You can't fake it. That is, I suppose you could take a stone and start carving, if you know ancient Aramaic as it was written down 3,000 years ago, and so on. But it's too preposterous. When archaeologists with no ax to grind dig into the ground, they date things with care. Some of them are very skeptical of Scripture, obviously, in Israel. There are, we learn, Bible minimalists and Bible maximalists. And the minimalists say, "The Bible is not to be relied on. It's just a religious book, beautiful poetry, etc., well done; but not to be relied on as a scientific text." And they don't rely on it. Nevertheless, they don't find archaeology that disproves it, either.

But the Bible maximalists say, "Use the Bible when you dig because it will tell you where to dig." And frankly, I've heard a story of farmers who plant the tamarind tree according to where the Bible says it will grow well, and they prosper doing that. So, you have both views. And I'm bringing that out purposely because it's not partisan. The Bible seems to be a truthful book, as far as that goes. And they use it in that manner.

Now archaeology again simply establishes primacy like nothing else. If I dig in my yard and I find a tomahawk, I don't think it's from an ancestor of mine that is a white European immigrant. I know it's from the Indians. I know that. Well if I find written material in ancient Hebrew and Aramaic, I know

Whose Land Is It?

it's from the Jews, if that happens in Israel. And the whole world knows it. And the whole world respects the idea of prior title.

You know, when you buy a piece of property, you buy title insurance with it. What is that stuff? The insurance company guarantees the title to be, in effect, an original. You have the title to the property, and there is no prior title. They will research the title to be sure there are no other claimants. And if somebody does step forward, you pay the premium. The insurance company will go to battle with him and defend your interest, or in the end he'll pay you off, or whatever. But, they guarantee that your title holds sway. Well, there's no better title than a piece of archaeology in the earth. There's just nothing to replace it. People's lawyers come and go, and draw titles through all many centuries. But archaeology is foolproof. It's just as simple as that.

Now, the last point. Land conquered. It goes to the last conqueror. Those are the rules in this world. There has to be some rules. That's the most convenient thing. Frankly, land in Israel goes to the guy with the most guns. That's what has happened for centuries. That's what happened here in America. Once again, we immigrants have no real right to this land, other than our soldiers have won it in battle.

There was a World Court proceeding over Danzig,

Whose Land Is It?

which is a country that was in an unfortunate location at the end of WWII. They were sort of Polish and German both. They spoke the German language. They had Polish customs. They were located between those two nations. The Germans swept over them on the way to Russia. Then the Russians swept over them on the way to Germany at the end of the war. They wanted to be Poles rather than Germans. They wanted to be on the winning side, and they took the case to the World Court. And the World Court looked at the case and decided it in their favor. They are Poles now because the Russians, who were allied with Poland, were the last conquerors. It's just that simple. Now if we apply the rule to the United States – and nobody's calling Texas Mexico – we were the last conquerors. Nobody's calling Louisiana France. We purchased it. We were the last through there.

Then why wouldn't we do that with the West Bank and Israel, let's say, the so-called West Bank? The Jews conquered it last in the Six Day War in 1967. There's no question of that. The whole world saw that. Why are they called occupiers since their archaeology's right there in the ground? Why are they considered sojourners in the land when all of the proofs I've given and obtained today are known by all sides?

Perhaps the media doesn't know what I'm saying, but they ought to. They're deciding just a little bit

Whose Land Is It?

too much about the situation. And you've got most of the world up in arms about Israel, and the whole thing is terribly unfair. It's unfair to boycott a democracy. It's unfair to divest from a going[?] free country in favor of a dictatorship.

I guess I hardly have to put these things into words. But I challenge anybody to have me come and speak and say these things on a university campus, in a church, in a civic meeting. I am open and I will not charge any fee or travel expense to do that. I feel this is a necessary thing to say everywhere as long as I can.

Once again, the prior title, the history, the archaeology, and the military conquest all point to Jewish ownership of the land of Israel. There's no other question, and no other claim that can hold up to the Jewish claim, and it's time that the whole world realized it and gave a chance to this brave young democracy to overcome the evil that's going on in that land every day, right now, while we read these things in the media.

The View from Palestine

Transcript from the Original
Zola Levitt Presents Program

Zola Levitt

The View from Palestine

> This is a transcript of a spoken lesson, and we wanted to remain faithful to the verbal text. Slight editings for clarity have been made. Allowances should be made for the fact that spoken language reads differently than literary text.

The View from Palestine

Key:

Zola = Zola Levitt
HA = Hanan Ashrawi
JF = Joseph Farah
EC = Ergun Caner

Part I

Zola: On our past trip to Israel, we had a rather exciting adventure. We received an offer that we could go with our American crewmen only, not the Israelis, to the checkpoint at Ramallah and meet a friendly Palestinian crew (and they were friendly and professional), and they would take us into Ramallah where we could observe firsthand what was going on in the West Bank, Arafat's headquarters, and especially we could interview Hanan Ashrawi, who is a major spokesman for the PLO, the Palestinian Authority. She was a member of their national parliament, and so forth, a very outspoken critic of Israel, and one of the important voices in this ongoing controversy.

We took them up on it. We crossed through the checkpoint – rather intense and pressuresome – and we met with Mrs. Ashrawi.

She talked to me, and it's just her point of view, obviously. In some ways I found myself disagreeing with her way of characterizing things, and I knew that would probably be the case. I didn't

The View from Palestine

want to comment personally. I didn't want to be Zola versus Dr. Ashrawi.

So we have friends over here who are Arab Christians. She's an Arab Christian. So we took the tape of our interview to two men (very trustworthy on Arab Christian affairs, and also on the situation in the Holy Land), and that is Dr. Ergun Caner, who is a professor at Criswell College. He's been on our program before. And Joseph Farah, a journalist. He is the editor of *World Net Daily*, a computer page – one of the largest news pages on the computer, very important. And he also is an Arab Christian. And what we did was take the points she made, and give them to Dr. Caner and to Joseph Farah and let them comment. And we'll let you be the judge. So we started this way....

Zola   Dr. Ashrawi, I really appreciate you taking time to talk with us this morning.

HA   My pleasure. Call me Hanan, please.

Zola   I will, and I know you're very busy. I noticed in the paper the other day that, while Mr. Arafat made changes in the Palestinian cabinet, you didn't approve entirely of the changes.

HA   No, I actually politely declined my appointment to the Cabinet one more time because I felt that this wasn't the real change that we

The View from Palestine

needed. We don't want change for change's sake. We want a qualitative difference.

Zola I guess there's a certain amount of corruption and problems in most governments, and you have always been a voice against that sort of thing.

HA Yes, I'm certainly for integrity in government, a system of government that is human-based and essentially democratic, and, of course, exercising the principle of accountability, and building efficient and professional and transparent institutions. I could recite the whole thing. I know we can do it. And I know we have the human capacity to do it. The problem is we need the will to carry out this change and to break the legacies that have brought about such tremendous suffering. And I feel the Palestinian people deserve it.

JF With regard to Hanan Ashrawi's comments about integrity – we have to give credit where credit is due. Hanan Ashrawi is one of the few people in the Arab world who has criticized Arafat and the PLO for corruption. And, of course, there's plenty of corruption to go around. Much of the money that has been funneled into the Palestinian Authority from Western Europe, from the United States, from Arab countries has found itself in the coffers

The View from Palestine

of people like Yasser Arafat in their Swiss bank accounts. Some estimate that the sums are in the billions of dollars. Ashrawi has been critical of that fact, and that's good. But I think she's soft-pedaling it a little bit. You can't have it both ways. You cannot build a Palestinian free state on a foundation of corruption. And that is what we have in Yasser Arafat's Palestinian Authority. Not only does the money come from foreign governments, the money also comes from a long history of narco-terrorism. The Palestinian Authority is deeply involved in drug trafficking internationally. They're involved in counterfeiting. They're involved in the kind of corruption that we here in the United States associate with gangland mob-style violence. They shake down their own citizens throughout the West Bank and Gaza. I'd like to see Hanan Ashrawi go a little bit further in her criticism of that corruption.

Zola   Yasser Arafat is an associate of yours. It appears he's a little bit frail at this time. Is his health in good order?

HA   His health is fine, given his age. He does take care of himself. He eats healthy. He rests enough. But he's under tremendous pressure. He's between a rock and a hard place, liter-

The View from Palestine

	ally, and is fighting once again for his own survival, as well as national survival. So he's in a very difficult and precarious situation.
Zola	Do you think he'll be re-elected?
HA	Oh yeah. You see, President Arafat has something that very few Palestinians have. He has a sort of symbolic, national historical dimension. So people are willing to forgive him his trespasses more than they are willing to forgive anybody else's trespasses. They look at the cabinet, they look at the people around him. They blame them, they hold them accountable. But somehow they keep exempting Arafat from this type of intrusive accountability.
Zola	I hear that he speaks Arabic with an Egyptian accent. He's originally Egyptian, and some object and some talk but...
HA	No. He's not originally Egyptian. He's Palestinian, definitely. But he spent part of his childhood in Egypt, and he's growing up here. He went to college in Egypt. So he has that Egyptian accent, yes. But it's something very superficial. You don't judge people by their accent.
JF	Hanan Ashrawi talks about the symbolic na-

The View from Palestine

ture of Arafat. There certainly is a lot of symbolism involved. I would suggest, however, that it's based more on myth than reality. She talks about the fact that Yasser Arafat went to college in Egypt, and she soft-pedals the idea that he's not a Palestinian. Well, the fact of the matter is he's not a Palestinian. This fact – that he was supported by Egypt, that he came from Egypt, that he was born in Egypt – is very important to understand the dynamic of the Palestinian/Israeli crisis. Because you have to be able to define who is a Palestinian to understand the nature of this struggle. If Yasser Arafat is a Palestinian, then any Arab who travels from any other country and visits or settles in that region can be considered a Palestinian. When you consider the fact that the Arab population is about 100 to 1 to Jewish population in the Middle East, you're not playing on an even playing field by any stretch of the imagination. So that's a fundamental problem that Israel is dealing with all the time. There are more Arabs living in that region today than ever before. Yet constantly what we hear is that conditions are so horrendous in the West Bank and the oppression for Arabs within Israel is so bad. The question is, if it's so bad, if conditions are that bad, why do the Arabs continue to migrate from every other Arab country in the world and even other Muslim countries? You'll

The View from Palestine

meet people who define themselves as Palestinians today in that region who come from Chechnya, who come from Bosnia, who come from Kosovo, who come from Iran – not even Arab populations, not even Arab people, and they're considering themselves Palestinians. That is a real problem, and it's one that's being soft-pedaled by Hanan Ashrawi.

Zola The situation with Iraq has some Americans wondering if this time he is sympathetic with Saddam. Where does the government stand?

HA I think the Palestinian people as a whole are sympathetic to the Iraqi people. There's a sort of affiliation and empathy with suffering. The Iraqi people are suffering in multiple ways. They're suffering because they have such a system as the Saddam regime, and they're paying the price of the dissidence of the Saddam regime. Of course, you would find sympathy among Palestinians, the Arab world, I think all people of conscience. They don't want to see innocent people suffer. At the same time, I don't think you will find anybody who supports Saddam Hussein, no. As a government, as a system of government, as a ruler, there's not much love lost. I think the emotional mistakes of the past are no longer in effect now.

The View from Palestine

JF   Hanan Ashrawi says that the Palestinian people identify with the Iraqi people because of the suffering that the Iraqi people have undergone. There's much more to it than that. One of the reasons that Yasser Arafat and so many of his entourage are supportive of Saddam Hussein (and, by the way, were supportive of Saddam Hussein in Iraq throughout the Persian Gulf War, are supportive of them now as the US is on the precipice of another war with Iraq), the reason they are so supportive is because Saddam Hussein has been a consistent supporter of the PLO and PLO terrorism throughout his reign of terror in Iraq.

Zola: We still continue our tours to Jerusalem on our normal schedule, and they are going on without event. Again, I've proved many times that it's more dangerous to stay home than to go to Israel, despite the way the news colors it. But there will come a day when it will be perfectly peaceful in Jerusalem, when we all live there in the kingdom to come. I refer you to Isaiah 11:9: *They shall not hurt nor destroy in all my holy mountain, for the earth shall be full of the knowledge of the Lord as the waters cover the sea.* Very encouraging. But on our last tour we had this adventure where we went to Ramallah. Now that's just near Jerusalem, almost a suburb. And drove in with a Palestinian crew to

The View from Palestine

interview Hanan Ashrawi, a Palestinian Authority spokesperson. And we took that tape to our friends, Dr. Ergun Caner and Joseph Farah, Arab Christians. Dr. Caner is not American, he is Lebanese to start with; and Farah was raised in Egypt. But they commented on what she had to say. So, picking right up again, here is Dr. Ashrawi.

Zola   The advertisement that ran recently with a number of signatories, including yourself, about the suicide bombings. You said they're counterproductive. Still, there is here and there an incident. What's your position on this?

HA   I believe that targeting innocent civilians, regardless of nationality, race, color, ethnic origin, creed, religious affiliation, is something that is unacceptable, morally reprehensible, and should be stopped immediately. And I believe that regardless of the motives, the justifications, the feelings of the perpetrators, that there is no way in which that should be accepted. So I think we have to deal with this issue seriously, publicly. We have to launch a debate, a dialogue on this issue. We cannot justify the targeting of Israeli civilians by saying our civilians have been systematically targeted by Israel. Because what you condemn when it's done unto you, you do not adopt as a means of retaliation and revenge.

The View from Palestine

EC Thankfully, we're finding some Palestinians who are against the *jihadim*, against these acts of public suicide bombings. The sad thing is almost all of the recent polls indicate that the majority, if not a significant number of Muslims, believe that suicide bombings are not only necessary, but actually morally sound acts in defense of what they believe to be the truth.

Zola The peace process, such as it is, it's had ups and downs. But what changes would you make to bring peace?

HA Well, I wish I were in control of all the factors. Unfortunately, I don't have the ability to re-appoint an Israeli government that would be committed to peace. I believe the greatest obstacle to peace is the nature of the Israeli government, the ongoing settlement activities, the extremism, the sort of built-in racism of the occupier, the mentality of the occupier, unbridled power, resorting to violence, thinking that military might can subdue a nation under occupation. So that is one essential ingredient. We have to appeal to the Israeli public to understand that the extremism and violence of this government is bringing disaster down on both our heads, on our side and on the Israeli side. But, at the same time, we

The View from Palestine

need to put our own house in order, to build our own institution of democracy, and at the same time to have third party participation. I believe this is a global endeavor. It is not bilateral. In this asymmetry of power, you do need international participation, positive intervention to prevent further deterioration and to launch a peace process that would have substance and credibility and have applicability on the ground.

JF Well, as usual, Hanan Ashrawi blames the Israelis for being THE obstacle to peace in the Middle East. And of course that is terribly unfair. Any impartial observer will look at the concessions that were made, particularly through the Barak administration, and recognize that clearly Yasser Arafat and the Palestinian Authority were not willing to negotiate in good faith at all, that their real objectives are the destruction of the State of Israel, and that no interim grounds would ever be acceptable to them. Only for Western audiences does this idea that the Palestinians want to create their own separate state side-by-side with Israel living in peace, only in Western audiences is that message even disseminated. It goes back to a strategy that was developed back in 1970 when a high-level PLO delegation went to Hanoi, went to North Vietnam. They asked the Vietnamese why the

The View from Palestine

Western world looked at the Vietnamese struggle as a national liberation movement, and looked at the Palestinian movement as a terrorist movement. The North Vietnamese gave them some very candid advice about how to deal with that. One of the objectives was this idea of creating interim steps to their ultimate objective, which has always been the destruction of Israel; and the Vietnamese gave them the advice to come up with a plan for their own state as an interim step that would define them then as a national liberation movement. And that's what they have done. It's been a propaganda ploy for the last 32 years, developed with the North Vietnamese back in 1970.

Zola What is the real history of the Palestinian people in this land?

HA We go back centuries. Actually, if you want, we go back to the Canaanites. So the Palestinians are the longest-standing ongoing historical human tradition in Palestine. Of course, we are also a mix of so many tribes that came into Palestine. My family has been here for centuries. Most people trace their families in centuries and thousands of years. It's amazing for people to tell us you're an accident of history, and re-define our being,

The View from Palestine

our culture, our history, our sense of value. From being the people of the land, and then we are told, no, this land has to be given away in accordance with the Bible or something. If you reorganize the world in accordance with the Bible, you'd be in serious trouble.

EC There are three fundamental points that I think are necessary to make here historically. Number one is the ludicrous statement about a Palestinian nation. There has never in the history of civilization been a Palestinian nation, ever. The human cry for a Palestinian state did not even begin until 1948, when Israel became a nation itself. One of the things that I state in public debates is that I believe the Palestinians should have as much land as they have ever had historically, which, of course, is none. She believes that she's a Christian, and as a professed Christian she should understand that God made a covenant with Israel. This is fundamentally important. The Land was given by God to the Jews. And as a Palestinian Christian, she must know her Old Testament on this.

The final thing I want to ask is, "Why, in the midst of all of this cry for peace, why has not one Arab nation offered a parcel of their land to give to the Palestinians?" And, of course, the answer is this is not as much about giv-

The View from Palestine

ing the Palestinians a nation as much as it is the taking away of a nation from Israel.

JF Hanan Ashrawi, I believe, is someone who believes principally in freedom and democracy and those kinds of things, and I give her high marks for sincerity. But when she talks about the Palestinian people retracing their history to the Canaanites, she loses me. When she talks about the fact that Palestinians have the longest-standing tradition of humanity in that region of the world, again she loses me. We don't need to go back thousands of years to see who's been living in that part of the world. We can go back to the turn of the 20th century and look at what the population levels were. At that time when the area that we call Palestine was ruled by the Islamic Ottoman Empire, the majority of the population in Jerusalem, the overwhelming population in Jerusalem, was Jewish. The second highest population level was among Christian Arabs. And Muslims, who now tell us that Jerusalem is the third holiest site in all of Islam, actually were a very small minority of about 10% of the population. So it's very hard for me to look at what Hanan Ashrawi says about this longstanding tradition in the region. The truth of the matter is the Arab population has been on the increase ever since the turn of the 20th century, and they came

The View from Palestine

for two principal reasons: they came, interestingly enough, because of the economic activity stirred by Jewish immigration in the region, and because of the freedom that the Jews brought with them.

Zola Among our audience, there are a number of Bible believers, since you bring up the Bible. What is the history of the Jews in the land? Because they would hold that the Jews have been here since the Canaanites, as well.

HA Oh, the Jews came and went in many ways, and they were part of the pluralism and the diversity of this culture. There were many Jews who stayed, but it hasn't been a Jewish state, so to speak. It's been an Arab state for centuries. We, as Christians, and I'm very proud of my culture as a Christian, we go back to the earliest Christian tradition. So, I'm amazed when I hear people in the West or in the Bible Belt telling me what I should be, or imposing on me their interpretations of Christianity, which, after all, is a Middle Eastern religion. We practice it, we exercise it, we live it as a living culture. It's part of our identity. It is my history. It is my culture. It's part of my authenticity. The same way as the land is my history, and my culture. After all, we belong to a dual tradition, the peasant cul-

The View from Palestine

ture and tradition which makes the land sacred. And, of course, the birth of the three monotheistic religions, and so that gives it additional value and spirituality. So both merge in my culture. And I feel that I'm very privileged of this culture, of this pluralism, and tolerance and diversity. The problem comes when you transform a religion into a national cause and identity, and you try to claim exclusivity, and you expel the rightful people of the land in order to reclaim, and you bring in people from all over the world thinking that this is your birthright, when we have land deeds, we have history, we have ongoing reality that tells you this is ours. So, it's not a question of deed, it's a question of continuity. It's a question of a longstanding ancient culture. We are proud of our heritage. We are a proud nation, after all. And we will not be dislodged or dispossessed. That's why the tragedy of '48 meant so much to the Palestinians, because when you dispossess, disperse, and exile a nation that has lived with the land on the land, with a sense of family and community as being the main source of security. And we certainly are a stationary people. Our metaphor is very organic. We are deep-rooted. So when you uproot a nation, you rob it of all its sense of security, of its identity, of its community. This is the worst tragedy that can befall a nation. This is what

The View from Palestine

happened to the Palestinians.

EC   Well, obviously, for a people to be dislodged and dispossessed, they must have at one time been lodged and have possessed the land. But again, they didn't claim land or statehood before 1948. It is only now, after. What you have is the Arab world has one common enemy and one common goal – the complete annihilation and dispossession of Israel.

Zola: Not everything in Ramallah was a peaceful conversation. We crossed a very tense border with a lot of soldiers. It's like two countries at war, almost, when you come to a place like that. And we looked at Arafat's headquarters, and boy, the news has not done justice to what's happened there. We got our own footage on that. We're going to continue next week with the rest of the interview with Mrs. Ashrawi and the commentary by Dr. Caner and by Joseph Farah. I should give Mrs. Ashrawi her due. She also holds a doctorate. She taught at the University of Virginia. This was an interview where I received information I didn't know. And, like I say at the beginning, some of it I obviously don't agree with. But I thought I would step aside and not be the commentator. I usually am the commentator. But there are more expert people; and more so, they are her peers. Dr. Caner and Joseph Farah are exactly equal to her in that they are Ar-

The View from Palestine

abs, Christians, knowledgeable on the Middle East, and so on. And it's not a matter of opinion when it comes to the history or the facts. There's some opinion in any interview. We had them look at all of what she said, and comment accordingly. So, you be the judge. We did not censor anything that she said, and we've only edited for time considerations, not for content. And you're getting her full testimony and the replies by our experts. So, join us again next week. We'll continue this, and as you do so, more than ever, pray for the peace of Jerusalem.

Part II

Zola: Shalom. Hello again. We're continuing from last week. I think it's a very interesting and educational sort of program. On our last Israel tour, we had the opportunity to travel into Ramallah in the West Bank, which turned out to be the de facto Palestinian capital, if you will. That's where Arafat's headquarters are. And that's where we encountered a Palestinian film crew who were very courteous and professional. They took us to Dr. Hanan Ashrawi who is one of the Palestinian spokespeople. She's recently appeared in the United States, at the University of Colorado, I believe. She has before been a speaker here and taught at the University of Virginia. She gave us her view of the whole controversy going on in Israel. I listened politely. I did not interrupt or argue. Much of what she said is worth

The View from Palestine

hearing, and quite truthful. And other things are more controversial. And rather than being the spokesperson, we turned this footage over to two Arab Christian experts that we know. Dr. Ashrawi is an Arab Christian, and her peer, Dr. Ergun Caner, an Arab Christian, is a professor at Criswell College in Dallas; and then Joseph Farah, the editor of *World Net Daily*, a very knowledgeable Arab American Christian. Dr. Caner was raised as the son of a muezzin and as a Muslim, and then converted to Christianity. Joseph Farah was raised in an Arab Christian family. They differ in that respect. But at this point they are her peers and they commented on what she said. So now, picking up from where we left off last week, we'll hear from Dr. Ashrawi and then our commentators.

Zola   I read an article about you in an Anglican magazine describing your Christian testimony. It was excellent. On the *McNeil Lehrer Report* you made a statement that was curious. You said, "Jesus Christ was a Palestinian prophet, born in Bethlehem in my country." I wondered about that.

HA   Well, of course, He was born Jewish but He was Palestinian because He was born in Palestine. There are still many Jewish Palestinians. Those who choose to be Israeli are Israeli Jews, but there are many, mostly outsiders, who are Palestinian Christians, and

The View from Palestine

some who are puristic. But I felt that He belongs to my heritage, to my past. And we are the most ancient Christian community. He was a Palestinian, He was a Jew, and He became a Christian.

JF We have to deal with the issue of Hanan Ashrawi's Christian testimony a little bit. Number one – I think it's very important to understand, particularly for American audiences, that when people in the Middle East talk about themselves as being Christian, often now what they're talking about really is a form of cultural Christianity, rather than a deep-seated belief of the heart. And I believe that's where Hanan Ashrawi is coming from in defining herself as a Christian Arab. She talks about Jesus Christ being a Palestinian, and her rationale for that is that he was born in Palestine. Well, that's kind of ludicrous, because the first time the term "Palestine" is used was in 70 AD when the Romans renamed Israel Palestine as a way of adding insult to injury after they destroyed the temple and committed genocide against the Jews. So the idea that Jesus Christ was a Palestinian is very much stretched.

Zola What would happen, this is almost a fantasy, but let's say a two-nation solution is formed,

The View from Palestine

something like that; and Palestine would have a nation, have control, and as a matter of fact, since they're largely Muslim, they begin to act like a Muslim government and tell you to cover your hair, this sort of thing?

HA Historically, Palestine has always been one of the most tolerant, open, liberal, and pluralistic societies in the Arab world, and in the region.

EC Tolerant? Open? I wonder how she would classify the Six Day War? Was that tolerant? How about Yom Kippur? We hear in our culture today, especially in America in this winter, that we should not bomb during Ramadan, that we should not bomb during any festival during Muslim holy days, because this would offend them worldwide. How offensive was it for them to pick the High Holy Day, the Day of Atonement, for them to bomb Israel?

JF Hanan Ashrawi says that Palestine has always been one of the most open, liberal, pluralistic, and tolerant societies in the region. I don't know what time frame Hanan Ashrawi is talking about, but first of all, there has never been a Palestinian state. There has never been a society, a self-governing entity known as Palestine in the history of the world. So you first of all have to ask yourself, what

The View from Palestine

Palestine is Hanan Ashrawi talking about when she defines it that way? But if you want to use liberal, pluralist, tolerant and open societies as the standard for the Middle East, there is only one – and it's the State of Israel. It's the only democratic country in the region. There are 23 Arab and Muslim states all bearing forms of totalitarian police states, and Israel is the only tiny bastion of democracy and freedom in the region.

HA   Islam has always been the most inclusive religion because it didn't come to deny previous religions. It came to affirm the two previous religions. My problem is with those and all religions, whether Islam, Christianity, or Judaism, who give themselves license to interpret in the most rigid dogmatic manner holy texts, and to use them to punish, to pound, to bash the others, and to negate and to deny the others. That is the problem. And you have those elements in all three religions. I believe that fundamentalism in Christianity is just as dangerous than it is in Islam, than it is in Judaism.

Zola   Well, I think Americans would say right there, "But wait a minute. Fundamental Christians have not attacked anyone or broken down the World Trade Center sort of thing."

The View from Palestine

HA Oh, well. It finds many different expressions. I mean, fundamental Christians also negate the validity and legitimacy of the others, which is very unchristian. Because Christianity is a very intolerant religion. And when fundamentalists tell me I have no right to exist as a Palestinian, regardless of my religion, and insist on negating my very rights (which is what's happening now), telling me that I should abandon my land, my history, my culture, my security, my life, for the sake of their interpretation of the Bible. This to me is the most dogmatic, rigid, and unchristian and inhuman way.

EC What I find fascinating is every time we have a released tape by Osama bin Laden or by any other Islamic leader, the first group to which they speak is not the infidel community. It's not the people of the great Satan. It is, in fact, speaking to other Muslims, when they say, "You have been obliged to holy war." In other words, they don't see themselves as fundamentalists. They are purists. They believe the Koran. They believe the Hadith. They believe that once you've been obliged to holy war, you must fight holy war. They are not fundamentalists. Instead, they view these Muslims as bad Muslims.

Zola If a state is established, do you suppose that

The View from Palestine

Hamas and other militant groups will stop the resistance?

HA   Oh, yes. You see, the difference between Hamas and Islamic Jihad, as Palestinian organizations, as opposed to other Islamic organizations, is that they are linked to a certain national struggle. They're part of a struggle against the occupation. If you remove the occupation, you disarm and diffuse. They do not have a global message. They are not out there ...they've never carried out actions outside Palestine. They've never been out there trying to either proselytize or kill people, or impose Islamic agenda. That's number one. Two, we have sufficient democratic forces in Palestine in order to weaken extremism by democratic means. This is how we should deal with it. And the majority of Palestinians are committed to a two-state solution. They are committed to accepting the other, committed to this inclusive approach. And they don't want to destroy the State of Israel or replace the State of Israel.

JF   Hanan Ashrawi suggests that the Palestinian people support a two-state solution. In other words, the idea of a separate Palestine state and a separate Israel state living side-by-side in peace and harmony. I have carefully looked at every public opinion survey

The View from Palestine

done of Arabs in that part of the world, and I see no evidence to back that up. I wish it were so. But, the truth of the matter is, from my own personal anecdotal experience, the interviews I've conducted on the ground there, I see no evidence to suggest that. It's wishful thinking on her part.

Zola: Well, tours to the Holy Land continue as usual. There's some tension over there. It's not as dangerous as staying at home, and I've specified that many times. On our last tour we had this opportunity to go into Ramallah and talk with Dr. Hanan Ashrawi, one of the spokespersons for the Palestinian Authority. You've seen her on the news, I'm sure. We took that footage to Arab Christian experts of our own acquaintance, Dr. Ergun Caner and Joseph Farah, and they commented on what she said. I stepped out of it. I'm the neutral observer. I got the testimony from her and I took it to them, is all; and here is how it continued.

Zola   It's hard to believe in light of, well perhaps he's overly radical, but a Hamas leader said, "This militancy will continue until all the Jews leave the land of Palestine." And it's not a two-state solution.

HA   The majority of the Palestinians accept the two-state solution.

The View from Palestine

EC   Let me present you with a hypothesis. Let's say that a group in Idaho or Iowa or some small state sets up a compound, fences it in, and claims it to be the nation of this compound. To prove their point, they stop paying taxes. They set up their own banks. They set up their own systems. To further prove their point, when the police in that city or nearby that compound come by, they shoot them. They begin to go into the neighboring cities, and they bomb people. Some of them even strap bombs to themselves, walk into the stores and into the restaurants, and strap bombs on themselves. And they make the point, and they say, "We will not stop this until you recognize our compound as a separate sovereign nation." What would we do as Americans? What would our country do? But, in fact, that is what we are asking Israel to do. We are asking terrorists to set up their own country. We are allowing them to bomb Israel, to absolutely obliterate innocent civilians, and we ask them to think that these are acts of war and not terrorism. And then we are asking Israel to recognize them as a state, in other words, to benefit terrorism. Now, why would we not do that in America? Well obviously, two reasons come to mind. Number one, that's not the way a sovereign nation operates. But secondly, it rewards terrorism. Would we always suspect that they

The View from Palestine

might do more to get more land? Of course, and so should Israel. This is a time for Christians and evangelicals and for Jews to unite together and band together. We cannot reward terrorism. And we cannot reward acts of terrorism any more on our land than we would ask Israel to do on its.

Zola I can almost hear Americans saying, "But wait, Dr. Ashrawi. There are people in a hundred places in the world that are occupied. They don't actually kill the occupier."

HA There's no other occupier, no other military occupation....

Zola Well, how about in America? We have Native Americans on reservations. They're native to the land and yet they're occupied totally. But they don't come out and kill people.

HA That situation was resolved in a way which was entirely unfair to the indigenous Americans, but it hasn't been viewed as an occupation and a struggle for independence. Now, the Indian nations are seeking their recognition of their own identity and nationhood within the larger America. No, here we are seeking our freedom because we are under military occupation.

The View from Palestine

JF   One of the terms that defines the debate for Palestinian Arabs is this word "occupation," and we hear it over and over again, and we heard Hanan Ashrawi use it again. We say that there is only one country occupied in the Middle East, and it's the country of Lebanon, who's occupied by Syria. There is a form of occupation in Palestine today – and it's the occupation that Arafat is employing over the Palestinian people in the West Bank and Gaza, and so forth. All of that land was given to the Jews under the original UN Mandate. There is another Palestinian country today known as Jordan (it's always been a predominantly Palestinian population), and that really occupies most of the territory that was granted to the Arabs under the original UN Mandate. So this whole silly notion of occupation has to be turned around and stood on its head. Israel is not the occupier.

Zola   Alright now, in all fairness, I interview people on all sides of questions, and if I talk to an average M[m]ember of Knesset, I think he would probably say, "Look, we were here a long time ago. Palestinians are various Arabs from various states. We mean them no harm. We brought the 20th century to them, and so forth. But they just won't cooperate and won't live in a democracy, and we don't know which

The View from Palestine

way to turn."

HA But that's not the right view of history. Ask the Israelis you talk to, "When did you come to Palestine? When?" Those who were originally Palestinians are the minority within Israel. Most of them came from Brooklyn, from Moscow. These are people who came in with their different cultures and languages and so on, and religion became transformed into a political instrument in order to take over a land in which there were people who've been living continuously for centuries. We've been here for centuries. We didn't emerge only in response to the creation of the State of Israel.

JF Ashrawi says that, "We (meaning the Palestinian people) didn't just come about in response to the creation of the State of Israel." Only in response. And I think there's some candor there that I'd like to see from more of the Palestinian spokesmen. Indeed, what she's acknowledging is the fact that there's been this tremendous influx of Arab population in the region since the creation of the State of Israel. In fact, as I mentioned earlier, that influx began back as early as 1900 when the higher levels of Jewish immigration began. That is a reality that needs to be dealt with. Once again, we see that the folks we refer to as Palestinian are actually coming

The View from Palestine

from 22 Arab states, coming from non-Arab states, throughout the world. They're Muslims from Pakistan. They're Muslims from Indonesia. They're Muslims from all over the world, and today we call them Palestinian. And we're discussing giving them rights to a national homeland. It just doesn't make any sense.

Zola Now, Israeli politics is changing, too, as we speak. My goodness, this week not only did Arafat appoint new cabinet members, but half the Israeli government walked out.

HA Not half, a major portion.

Zola Not only are there changes in the Palestinian cabinet at this time, but in the Israeli Knesset. There's a sea change. A whole Labor Party walked out of the government. It's a minority of the government, but still they left. And this leaves the possibility of new elections coming up, quite a shakeup. It brings personalities out of the closet, so to speak. Just to ask, of course, you have Sharon in power. He wants to remain in power. Netanyahu's been suggested. Do you have a preference among these gentleman?

HA It's the lesser of two evils. I think they all be-

The View from Palestine

long to one camp. They may have internal domestic differences motivated by their own ambition (you know, who wants to outflank whom from the right). But most belong to the most extreme Zionist position, which is based on the negation of the other, which is based on the extension of the mentality of occupation, thinking that you can really defeat a nation, bent on getting its independence and freedom and dignity on its own land. And they both adopt military means and violence as a means of subduing a nation. To me, there is danger to Israel and to Palestine in having such an extremist government, because you also forgot one ingredient, you forgot Mofaz, who is known for his ruthlessness and violence, and the new defense minister; and of course they're courting Lieberman, who came from the ex-Soviet Union, who claims that God gave him all this land, therefore he has to carry out ethnic cleansing and kick out all the Palestinians and, of course, bomb Egypt and bomb Iran. So you have the most irresponsible, very dangerous combination of extremism. Not that the Labor Party made a lot of difference in that cabinet.

Zola Well, wait a minute. Barak was a Prime Minister of the Labor Party, and every American would like a clear answer to why, when he offered a viable Palestinian state in Washing-

The View from Palestine

ton, didn't Arafat say, "This is what we want, we'll take it"?

HA I'm glad you raised this question because there have been so many myths and distortions, and the American viewers have accepted a certain version that has nothing to do with reality. At Camp David there was no, as you say, "generous offer." There were discussions. There were initial ideas. There was nothing in writing. There were no agreements. There were just ideas that kept changing every day, saying how much land can Barak take away from the 22% which was the West Bank and Gaza to maintain more settlements? How much land can he take that would leave the Palestinian state territorially noncontiguous and therefore not viable? He wanted to annex areas within Jerusalem, around Jerusalem, Gaza and the West Bank. He wanted us to relinquish the right of return for all that.

And then to say this is the end of the conflict. These are not issues on which we can come to an agreement. These are ideas that need further development. And of course, we will not form a solution because the essential ingredient of justice is missing. So let's explore them further. There was no rejection and there was no offer.

The View from Palestine

EC The fundamental point that Dr. Levitt makes here, number one it must be stated, there was an offer made. And it must be stated that Arafat did in fact walk away. He would not sign an accord. He would not sign the agreement. He has a vested interest in revolution, but perhaps not as much in peace. He walked away.

JF Ashrawi says that during the Barak administration and during those negotiations, there was no rejection of a peace plan. In fact, she suggests there was no peace plan at all. That there was nothing really concrete put on the table, so there was nothing to reject in the first place. Now, as I understand it, she was not a part of those negotiations. She was not a part of the Palestinian Authority's negotiating team. So her understanding of what was happening would be based on the same kind of facts that are available to all of us, people who read newspapers and such. And people who do read newspapers and who are informed about those negotiations understand that there were indeed very, very concrete proposals, unbelievable concessions that were made by the Israeli leadership. In fact, the Israeli population was stunned that everything was put on the table, including Jerusalem was put on the table. The Temple Mount was put on the table. That is indeed why

The View from Palestine

Barak was ultimately rejected because this peace plan failed, and the Israeli population looked at that and said, "There is no way we could ever make these folks, the Palestinians, happy if they reject these kinds of concessions."

Zola: Well, that's the long and short of it. We gave Dr. Ashrawi an open mike, as they call it in the business. She was allowed to talk at length as she pleased. We didn't time it or say it was a 15-minute interview, or whatever, but just let her go ahead and tell us what she wanted to tell us.

We then took the tape to our experts, Dr. Caner and Joseph Farah, Arab Christians in America, and they commented on what she said. You be the judge. I'm in the middle. I just got the interview and transferred the tape, and that's all.

You know, there'll come a time in the future when we won't have to worry about these things, obviously. The Kingdom will come and it will be in the Holy Land and it will be in Jerusalem, and also in Ramallah. And there will be peace, as the Lord says in Isaiah 11:16: *There shall be a highway for the remnant of His people which shall be left from Assyria like as it was to Israel in the day that you came up out of the land of Egypt.* Isaiah 19 also describes this highway that runs from Arab nation to Arab nation right through Israel, through Syria, through Israel, to Egypt and back, therefore describ-

The View from Palestine

ing a peace.

We crossed a border so very treacherous, so dangerous, just to make this program. In that day we can go across national borders, never mind the border between Jerusalem and Ramallah. And at that time, we have the wonderful verse Isaiah 12:2: *Behold, God is my salvation; I will trust and not be afraid: for the Lord Jehovah is my strength and my song; He also has become my Salvation.*

Let me teach you something. In Hebrew, the word salvation is *Yeshua*. It's Jesus' name. It's what He was called in Israel, Yeshua. The verse that says Mary called his name Jesus because He brought His people salvation doesn't make any sense unless you use His real name, Yeshua. Then you would say, Mary called His name Yeshua, salvation, because He will bring His people salvation. Now it makes sense. So when it says that Jehovah also has become my salvation, the verse teaches that Jehovah becomes Jesus, and comes to the earth and brings Yeshua, salvation, to us.

Until that day comes, however, Ramallah and Jerusalem are awfully close together. And as you can tell from the testimony, there's still quite a bit of argument going on.

When I went to Ramallah, I was struck by the fact that we left our hotel and in 15-20 minutes we were at this checkpoint that looked like the Berlin Wall, for all that matter. Soldiers and confusion and people running here and there, and bombed-out cars, and all of the rest of it. I was struck by the

The View from Palestine

fact they are so close together. So when you think of these events in Ramallah, it is right on the border of Jerusalem. And when you do that, *Sha'alu Shalom Yerushalim,* pray for the peace of Jerusalem.

STUDY BOOK SERIES by Zola Levitt

THE MIRACLE OF PASSOVER
A complete explanation of the beautiful symbols and shadows of the Messiah which appear in this crown jewel of Jewish Holy Days. The true meaning of Communion as the Lord instituted it and as the Church practices it.

THE SPIRIT OF PENTECOST
From the fear and trembling of the Upper Room to the magnificent miracle of the coming of the Holy Spirit. An exciting presentation of the full meaning of "the birthday of the Church."

A CHRISTIAN LOVE STORY
The Jewish wedding customs of the Messiah's time and how He fulfilled them all in calling out His Bride, the Church. A new and deeper understanding of the bond between the Bridegroom and each believer – a spiritual "Love Story."

THE SIGNS OF THE END
The Messiah's own words of warning about the conditions that would prevail in the world at the end of God's plan. Are we now approaching the Great Tribulation and the return of our King?

GLORY: The Future of the Believers
The entire prophetic system explained for those who are going to live it! The Rapture, our time in Heaven, the Kingdom and eternity. Where we go from here. Our rewards, our eternal lives, our entire future.

THE SEVEN FEASTS OF ISRAEL
A complete explanation of the holy days God gave Moses on Mount Sinai, and how each was fulfilled by our Lord. Passover, Pentecost, Trumpets, Tabernacles, etc., fully discussed as to their hidden meanings in the Messiah. A very special section on how every baby in the womb develops according to God's system of the holy days.

THE SECOND COMING
The prime difference between the biblical faith and worldly religions is that with the Messiah we have a bright future. What we see is not all we get. The life in this world is of little importance to those who have been promised the Kingdom to come. The return of the King fully explained.

STUDY BOOK SERIES *continued*

SEVEN CHURCHES: Does Yours Fit In?
A refreshing and unusual perspective on the churches presented in Revelation 2 and 3. A Jewish Christian and Bible scholar, Zola looks at these earliest churches from the old Testament and Jewish traditional point of view. A highly interesting and most useful study, applicable to church life everywhere today.

HOW CAN A GENTILE BE SAVED?
Christians always ask Zola, "How did you come to the Lord?" Their real question is, "How can a Jew be saved?" He finally decided to make a biblical inquiry into how they got saved. The results are extremely thought-provoking.

IN MY FATHER'S HOUSE
The Lord said, "In my Father's house are many mansions... I go to prepare a place for you." An explanation of the incredible seven years we will spend as guests in heaven, in the Messiah's Father's house.

ISRAEL, MY PROMISED
Has God finished with the Jews? Are the modern Israelites the valid Chosen People of the Bible? A sensitive and very personal look at the land of our Lord, as seen today and as promised in the Kingdom.

To order additional copies of this transcript or for
a catalog of ministry materials, please contact:

Zola Levitt Ministries
P. O. Box 12268
Dallas, TX 75225
214-696-8844
www.levitt.com

To order additional copies of this transcript or for
a catalog of ministry materials, please contact:

Zola Levitt Ministries
P. O. Box 12268
Dallas, TX 75225
214-696-8844
www.levitt.com